ELEMENTARY MET

FOR

TYMPANI

THE TYMPANI

Kettle Drums (English)   Timpani or Timballi (Italian)
Pauken (German)   Timballes (French)
              Timbals or Atabales (Spanish)

Tympani ....A plural term, referring to two kettle drums.
Tympano ....A singular term, referring to one kettle drum.

TYMPANO NOMENCLATURE

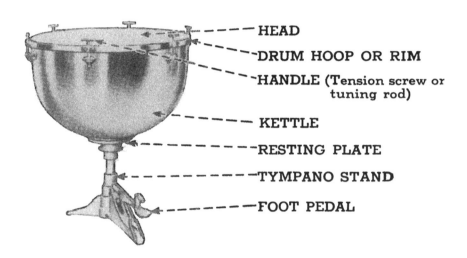

- HEAD
- DRUM HOOP OR RIM
- HANDLE (Tension screw or tuning rod)
- KETTLE
- RESTING PLATE
- TYMPANO STAND
- FOOT PEDAL

TYMPANO STICK

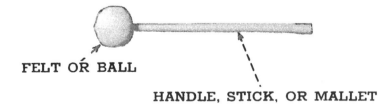

FELT OR BALL

HANDLE, STICK, OR MALLET

TYMPANI RANGE

Playing Position

The tympanist should assume a position facing the conductor. The small tympano is placed to the right-front of the player, and the large tympano to the left-front of the player. When the performer remains in a standing position the heads of the tympani should be approximately six inches below the waist line. However, many tympanists prefer to play while seated, and in this case the heads of the tympani should be approximately six inches above the seat. The kettles should be slanted toward the player, the amount of slant depending upon the actual height of the tympani.

Holding the Tympano Stick

Although the tympano stick is gripped and controlled chiefly by the thumb and first finger, with the thumb on top of the stick, the second and third fingers are closed around it also. The little finger does not touch the stick. The place on the tympano head which is most desirable as a spot for striking, is a point located about one-third of the distance between the drum hoop and the center of the head. Both sticks should strike on the head the same distance from the drum hoop, or the rim of the tympano. When the mallets are striking the same tympano head, they should be separated by one of the tuning rods, as this gives the player a greater space in which to play.

HOLDING THE TYMPANO STICK

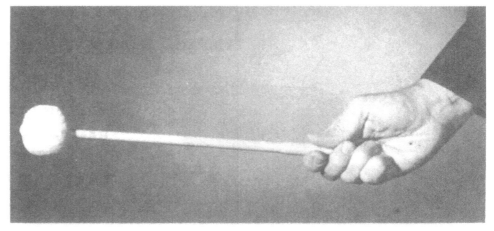

Tympani Tuning

Tympani usually are tuned in fourths or fifths, although occasionally they are tuned in other interval combinations (Richard Strauss employed thirds, and Beethoven even made use of octaves). When tuning by hand, opposite handles should be tuned simultaneously, and care should be taken to see that equal tension is given the head at each screw. In changing the pitch from a given pitch to a higher one, handles are turned to the right; in changing the pitch from a given pitch to a lower one, handles are turned to the left.

When tuning by pedal, the pitch is raised by pressing the pedal down, and lowered by bringing the pedal up. However, each head must be set to an even tension by the handles (tension screws or tuning rods) before using the pedals for tuning.

Preparatory Studies

SMALL TYMPANO

Whole note (o) = Four counts   Whole rest (☰) = Four counts

R = Right Stick   L = Left Stick

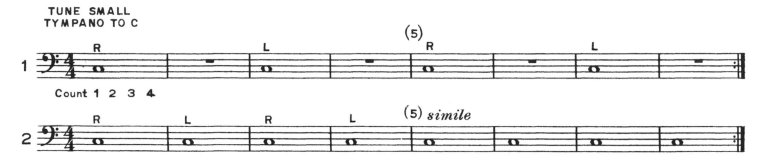

LARGE TYMPANO

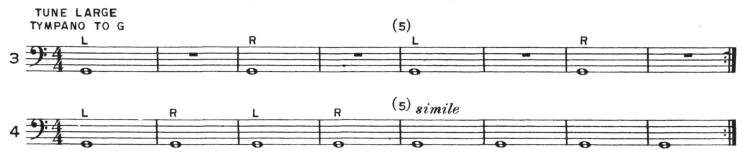

INTRODUCING HALF NOTES AND HALF RESTS

Half note (♩) = Two counts   Half rest (☰) = Two counts

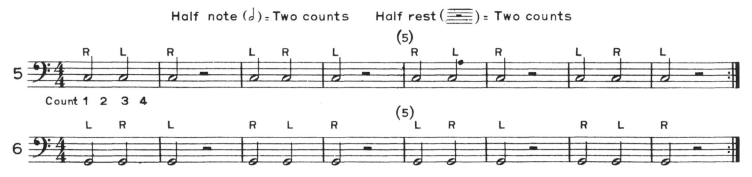

INTRODUCING QUARTER NOTES AND QUARTER RESTS

Quarter note (♩) = One count   Quarter rest (𝄽) = One count

TYMPANI STUDY - From Right to Left

In passing from the small tympano (which is placed on the right-front) to the large tympano (which is placed on the left-front), lead with the left stick.

TYMPANI STUDY - From Left to Right

In passing from the large tympano (which is placed on the left-front) to the small tympano (which is placed on the right-front), lead with the right stick.

HALF NOTE EXERCISE

QUARTER NOTE EXERCISE

Basic Studies

In order to pass in the most natural manner from one tympano to another tympano, begin all even groups of notes (two, four, six, etc.) with the hand in the direction of which it is necessary to go; in the case of one note, or uneven groups of notes (three, five, seven, etc.) begin with the hand opposite the direction of which it is necessary to go.

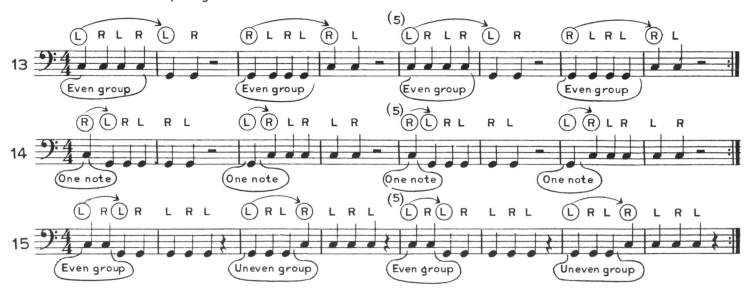

989-48

Developing the Stroke

Introducing 2/4 Time (Meter)

EXERCISE

EXCERPTS from the LINZ SYMPHONY

MOZART

Introducing ¾ Time (Meter)

EXERCISE

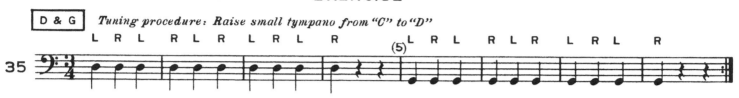

EXCERPTS from the OXFORD SYMPHONY

HAYDN

Tuning Technique

(For Small Tympano)

DIATONIC STUDIES

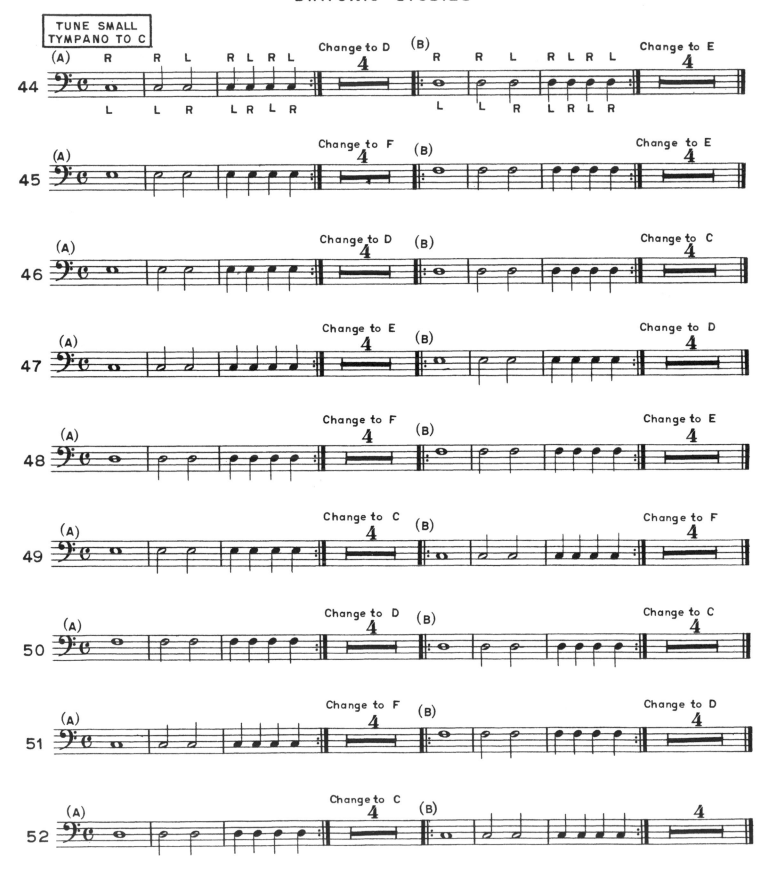

Tuning Technique
(For Large Tympano)

DIATONIC STUDIES

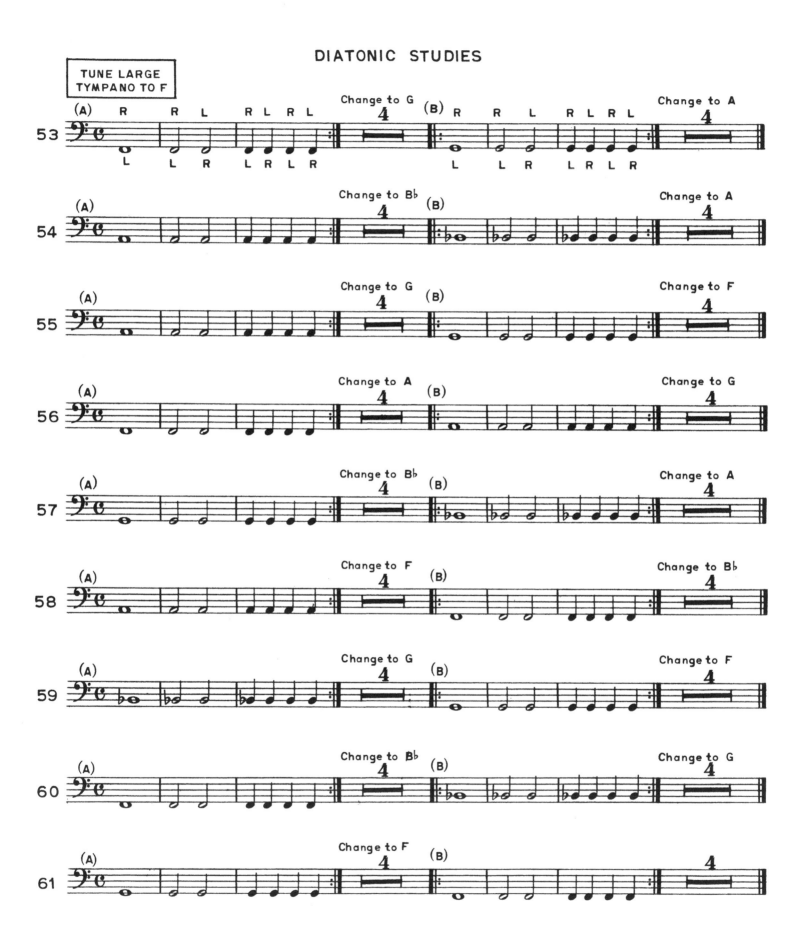

Tuning Technique
(For Tympani)

BY INTERVALS of a PERFECT FOURTH

BY INTERVALS of a PERFECT FIFTH

989-48

Tuning Technique
(For Tympani)

CHROMATIC STUDIES

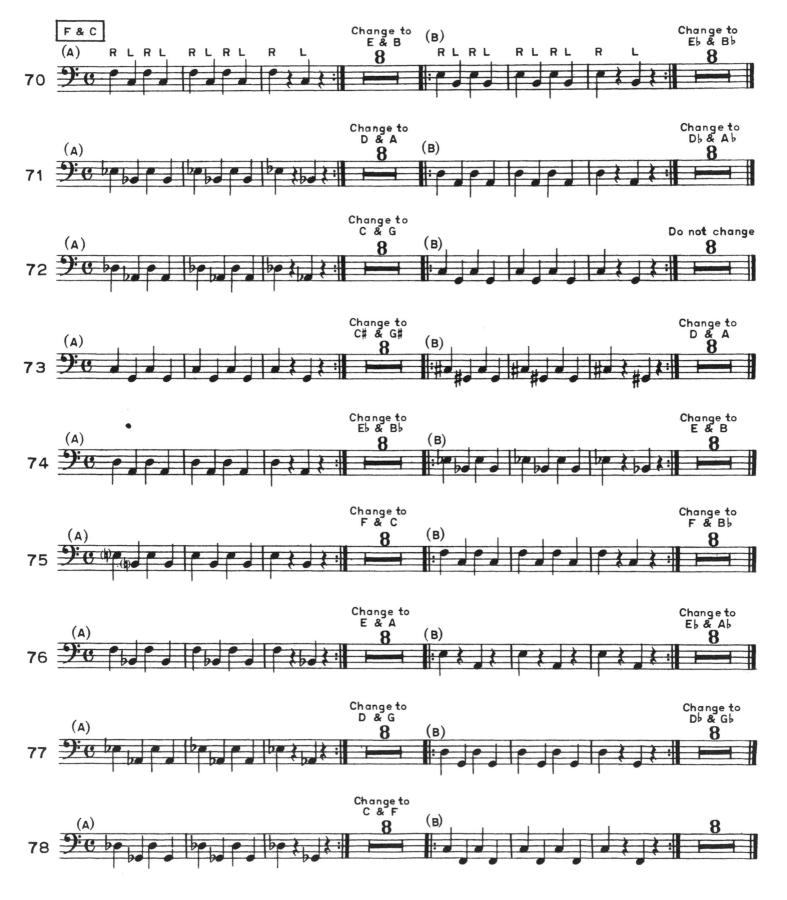

Pedal Practice

Tuning Exercises for Pedal or Single-Screw Machine Tympani Only

Small Tympano

DIATONIC STUDIES

CHROMATIC EXERCISE

Pedal Practice

Tuning Exercises for Pedal or Single-Screw Machine Tympani Only

Large Tympano

DIATONIC STUDIES

CHROMATIC EXERCISE

Introducing Eighth Notes

QUARTER and EIGHTH NOTES ALTERNATED

The EIGHTH REST

EIGHTH NOTES and EIGHTH RESTS in 4/4 TIME (Meter)

TECHNIC BUILDER

FOUNDATION STUDY

From DON GIOVANNI OVERTURE

MOZART

From the OVERTURE to IPHIGENIA IN AULIS

GLUCK

EIGHTH NOTES in ¾ TIME (Meter)

From SYMPHONY No.7

HAYDN

ABBREVIATED MARKINGS of EIGHTH NOTES

From the FIFTH SYMPHONY

BEETHOVEN

From SYMPHONY No.7

HAYDN

From LEONORE OVERTURE No.1

BEETHOVEN

INTRODUCING the DOTTED QUARTER NOTE FOLLOWED by an EIGHTH NOTE

EXERCISE

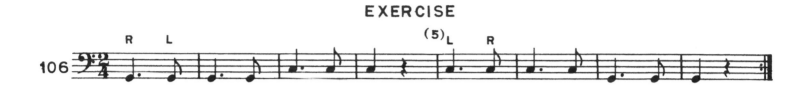

RHYTHMICAL STUDY

TECHNIC BUILDER

From LA CLEMENZA DI TITO OVERTURE

MOZART

From DON GIOVANNI OVERTURE

MOZART

From IDOMENEUS OVERTURE

MOZART

Introducing Triplets

Three notes played in the time value of two of the same kind of notes are known as a triplet. The most common type of triplets is that represented by three eighth notes. Usually a triplet is indicated by a figure 3 written above or below it.

QUARTER NOTES and TRIPLETS ALTERNATED

EIGHTH NOTES and TRIPLETS ALTERNATED

From the ACADEMIC FESTIVAL OVERTURE

BRAHMS

From the FIFTH SYMPHONY

BEETHOVEN

From HULDIGUNGSMARCH

WAGNER

Introducing ⅝ Time (Meter)

Eighth note (♪)= 1 count   Quarter note(♩)= 2 counts

EXCERPTS from the MILITARY SYMPHONY

HAYDN

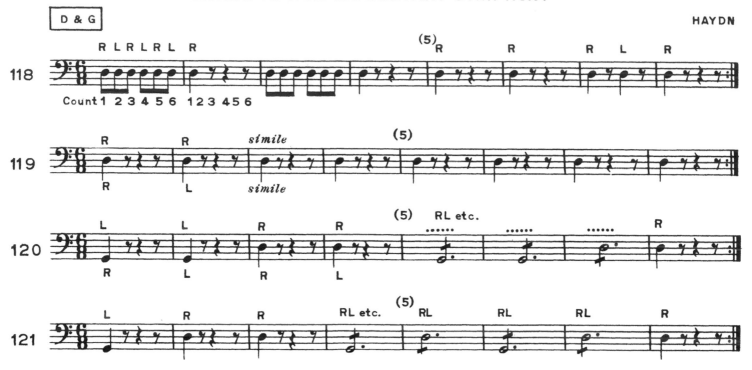

EXCERPTS from the SURPRISE SYMPHONY

HAYDN

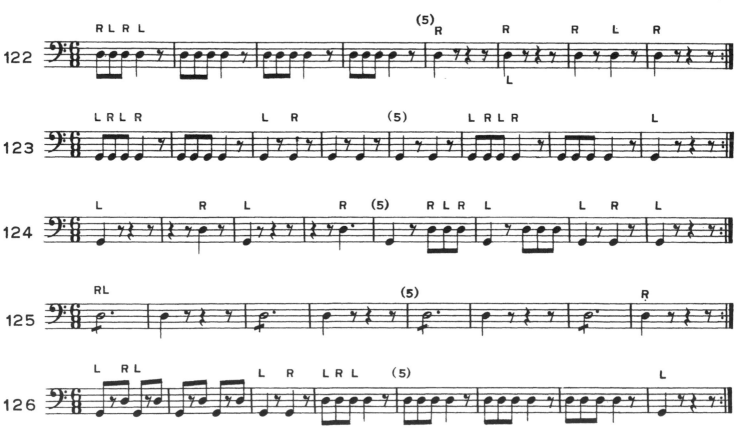

989-48

EXCERPTS in ⅝ TIME from the ITALIAN SYMPHONY

MENDELSSOHN

INTRODUCING SIXTEENTH NOTES

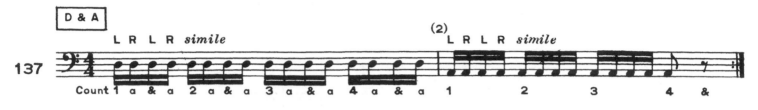

QUARTER and SIXTEENTH NOTES ALTERNATED

RHYTHMICAL STUDY

ABBREVIATED MARKINGS of SIXTEENTH NOTES

From the OVERTURE to ZAMPA

HEROLD

From the SECOND SYMPHONY

BEETHOVEN

From the Symphonic Poem BLANIK

SMETANA

INTRODUCING the DOTTED EIGHTH NOTE FOLLOWED by a SIXTEENTH NOTE

Count 1 & a 2 & a 3 & a 4 & a

EXERCISE

From the FIFTH SYMPHONY

BEETHOVEN

From the HAFFNER SYMPHONY

MOZART

From the OVERTURE to IPHIGENIA IN AULIS

GLUCK

From the JUPITER SYMPHONY

MOZART

Introducing the Roll (or Tremolo)

Use alternate (1) left and right strokes, or (2) right and left strokes in playing the tympani roll (or tremolo). The double roll, such as employed on the snare drum, is not used in tympani playing.

BASIC EXERCISES
Small Tympano

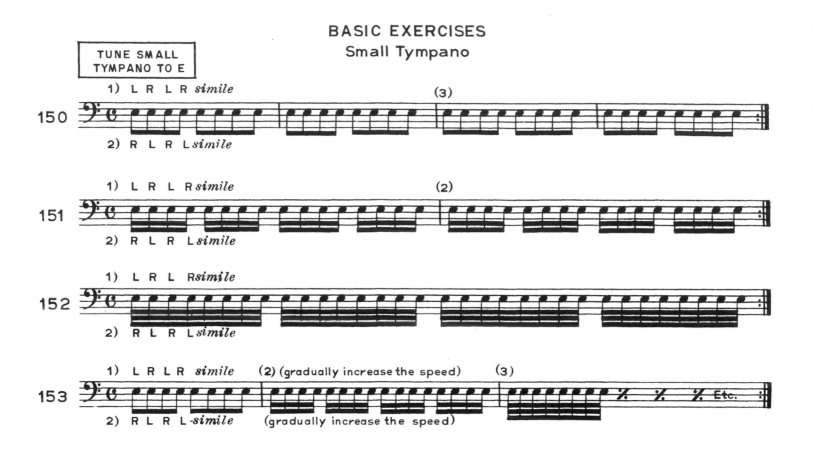

The Roll (or Tremolo) is Indicated in either of the following ways:

From the OVERTURE to ZAMPA

HEROLD

From the OVERTURE to TANNHAUSER

WAGNER

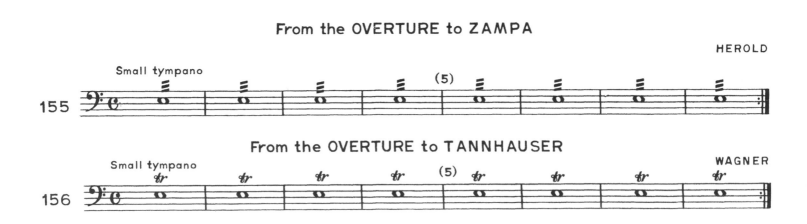

989-48

Developing the Roll (or Tremolo)

WHOLE NOTE ROLL

HALF NOTE ROLL

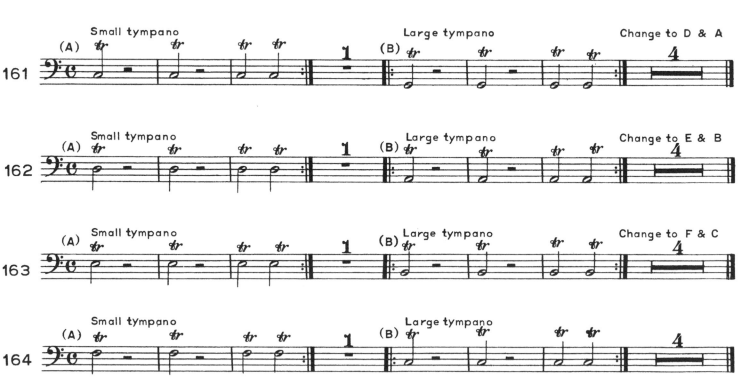

The Long Roll
(For Small Tympano)

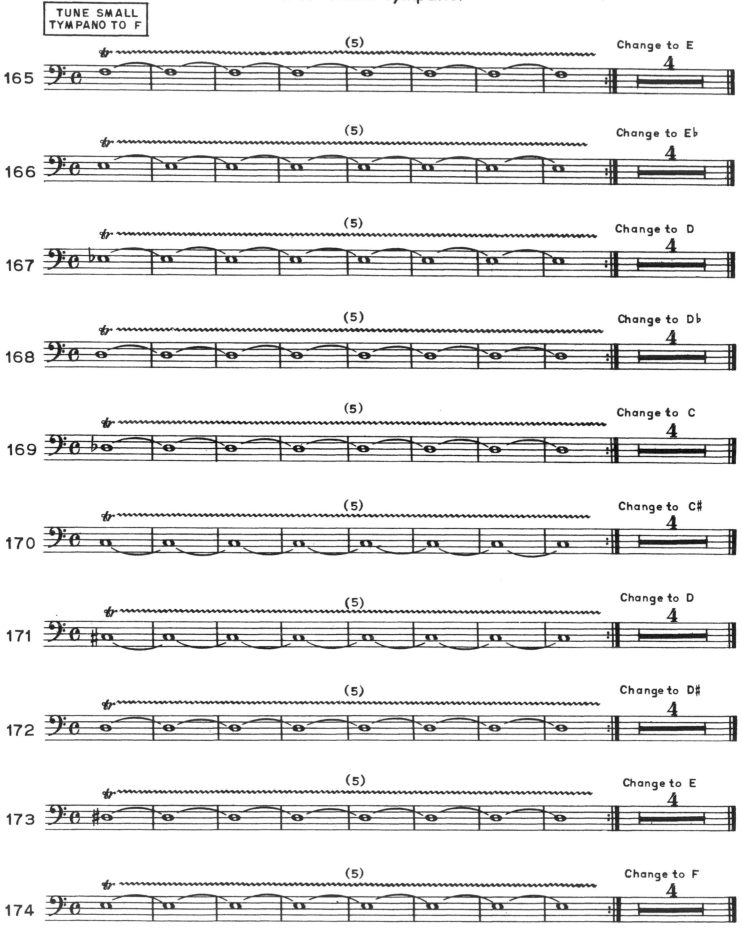

The Long Roll
(For Large Tympano)

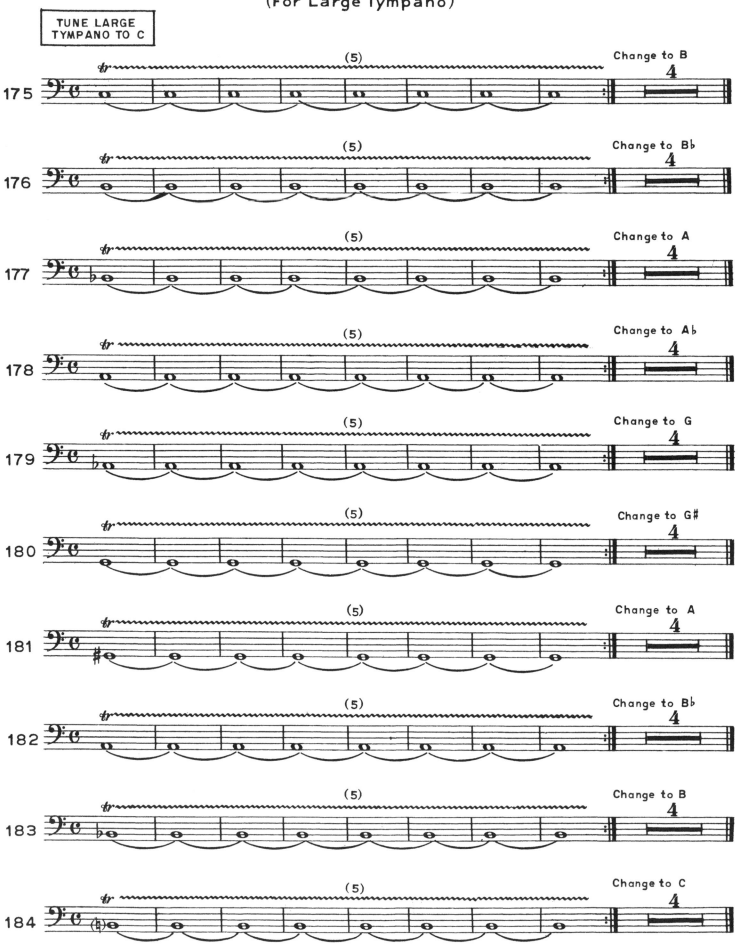

Introducing Dynamics

Dynamics: The marks indicating the degree of loudness or softness at which a musical composition is performed.

mf (*Mezzo forte*) Moderately loud   *mp* (*Mezzo piano*) Moderately soft
f (*Forte*) Loud   *p* (*Piano*) Soft
ff (*Fortissimo*) Very loud   *pp* (*Pianissimo*) Very soft
fff (*Forte possible*) As loud as possible   *ppp* (*Piano possible*) As soft as possible

The FORTE DYNAMICS

D & A

Practice (1) *mf* (2) *f* (3) *ff* (4) *fff*

The PIANO DYNAMICS

Practice (1) *mp* (2) *p* (3) *pp* (4) *ppp*

The "COPERTO" Effect

Coperto = Muffled. To produce the "Coperto" effect, place a cloth or handkerchief on the head at the opposite side to that being played upon. When the cloth or handkerchief is to be removed, the word "Scoperto" (meaning unmuffled or open) is employed.

Dynamic Development

The CRESCENDO
(Gradually louder)

Begin the pianissimo with the ball of each stick near the edge of the tympano and in producing each stroke keep the sticks close to the head of the instrument. Then, in order to gradually increase the volume of tone, slowly guide the sticks toward the center of the drum head and at the same time, raise them higher and higher with each succeeding stroke.

The DIMINUENDO
(Gradually softer)

Begin the fortissimo with the ball of each stick near the center of the tympano and in producing each stroke keep the sticks high from the head of the instrument. Then, in order to gradually decrease the volume of tone, slowly guide the sticks toward the edge of the drum head and at the same time, bring them closer and closer to the head of the instrument with each succeeding stroke.

FORTE-PIANO
(Attack each note strongly; then diminish instantly)

SFORZANDO
(Attack each note with great force; then diminish instantly)

CRESCENDO-DIMINUENDO
(Gradually louder; then gradually softer)

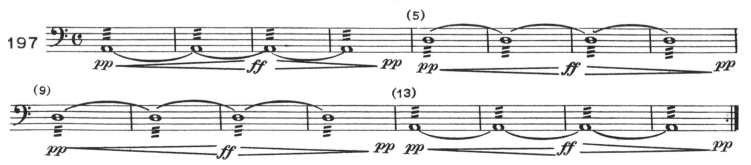

Orchestral Excerpts Employing the Roll

From LEONORE OVERTURE No.1

BEETHOVEN

From the ACADEMIC FESTIVAL OVERTURE

BRAHMS

From the MIDSUMMER NIGHTS DREAM OVERTURE

MENDELSSOHN

From the SECOND HUNGARIAN RHAPSODY

LISZT

From CORIOLAN OVERTURE

BEETHOVEN

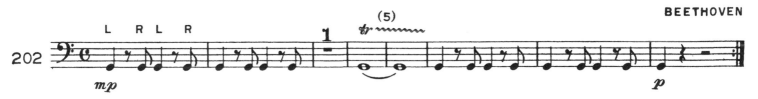

From the OVERTURE IN ITALIAN STYLE

SCHUBERT

28

From RUY BLAS OVERTURE

MENDELSSOHN

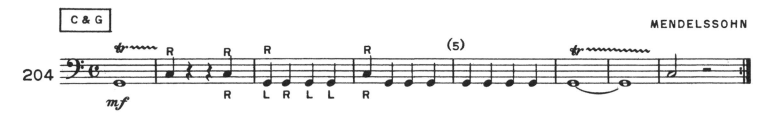

From LEONORE OVERTURE No.2

BEETHOVEN

From the SECOND HUNGARIAN RHAPSODY

LISZT

From the OVERTURE to DIE MEISTERSINGER

WAGNER

From the ACADEMIC FESTIVAL OVERTURE

BRAHMS

From the OVERTURE to DON GIOVANNI

MOZART

From OBERON OVERTURE

WEBER

From the OVERTURE to RIENZI

WAGNER

From the CLOCK SYMPHONY

HAYDN

From the SEVENTH SYMPHONY

BEETHOVEN

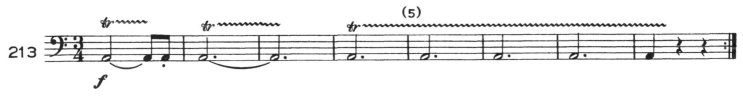

From the RED POPPY BALLET

GLIERE

989-48

From STRADELLA OVERTURE

Von FLOTOW

From the ZAMPA OVERTURE

HEROLD

From the CLOCK SYMPHONY

HAYDN

From the OVERTURE to RIENZI

WAGNER

From the HAFFNER SYMPHONY

MOZART

From SYMPHONY No.5

TSCHAIKOWSKY

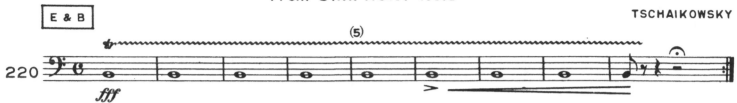

From the OVERTURE to TANNHAUSER

WAGNER

From the NEW WORLD SYMPHONY

DVORAK

From the OVERTURE to BARBER OF SEVILLE

ROSSINI

From the WILLIAM TELL OVERTURE

ROSSINI

From the WILLIAM TELL OVERTURE

ROSSINI

Grace-Note Embellishments

Grace notes are small ornamental embellishments, one or more of which precedes a main note.
A single grace-note is played preferably with the left stick, which is raised approximately one-third as high as the right stick. The stroke of each stick is started at the same time, but in the beat itself, the left stick must slightly precede the right stick.

STACCATO STROKES

DEVELOPING the STACCATO

Accent the first note of each pair; then strike the other note sharply and evenly, but with less force.

ACCENTED STROKES

Tuning-Changes

In the performance of orchestral and band music it frequently is necessary to change the pitch of either or both small and large tympano between movements or within the same movement of a musical score. Therefore, the tympanist must be able at all times to tune each tympano while the orchestra or band is actually playing. Such tuning, obviously, must be done in a quiet manner, and the pitch of the tympani should be tested by pressing on the head of each respective drum with the fleshy portion of the middle finger, and then lightly flipping the finger away from the instrument. In carrying out this procedure, the player should bend forward, in order to be in a position to readily discern the pitch of the instruments being tested.

Orchestral Excerpts Illustrating Tuning-Changes

MARCH from TANNHAUSER
WAGNER

DANSE MACABRE
SAINT-SAËNS

* Although there are actually more than twelve measures rest in the score itself, this number of measures is deemed sufficent for the student in making the tuning change.

36

989-48

Stopping (or Muffling) the Tone

Tympani tones should not necessarily be allowed to sound on until they die away, for often the continued vibrating of the heads results in a dissonant, unmusical effect. When it is desired that the tone be stopped (or muffled), the tympanist places his little finger on the tympano head (see illustrations), and then, one after the other, quickly drops each succeeding finger on it.

〰 = Stop (or muffle) the tone. Stop the tone with the same hand that made the beat.

Introducing Alla Breve (Cut) Time

Alla Breve (Cut) time is 4/4 time (meter) with TWO BEATS to the measure instead of four. It is indicated by the sign ₵.

EXCERPTS from JUPITER SYMPHONY
Illustrating Alla Breve (Cut) time

MOZART

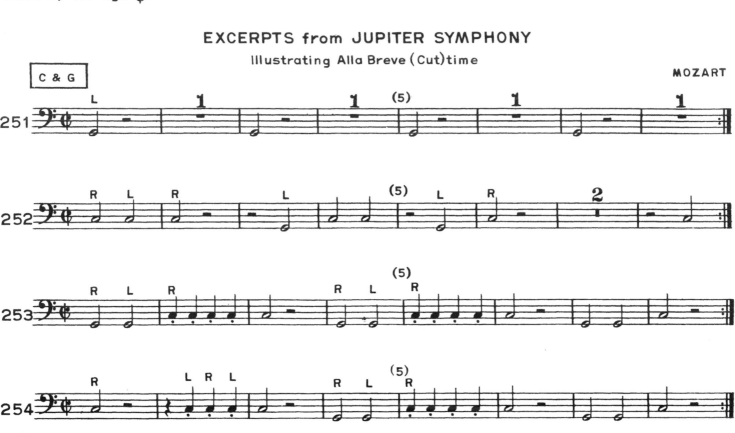

989-48

From the OVERTURE to DER FREISCHUTZ

WEBER

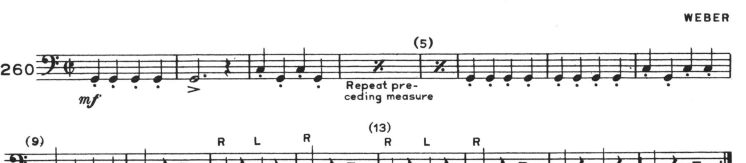

Repeat preceding measure

From the Symphonic Poem MAZEPPA

LISZT

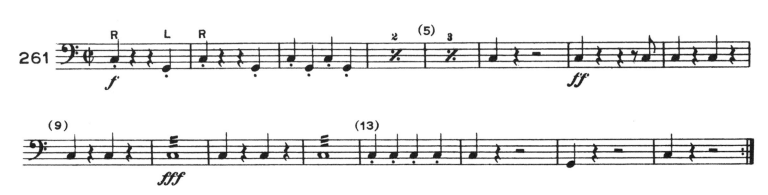

From RUY BLAS OVERTURE

MENDELSSOHN

Orchestral Studies

ALLEGRO from the FIFTH SYMPHONY

BEETHOVEN

* The tympanist must accustom himself to strict, accurate counting of the number of measures of "rest" which is indicated in nearly all tympani scores.

989-48

VORSPIEL from DIE MEISTERSINGER

WAGNER

MOLTO VIVACE from the OVERTURE to DER FREISCHUTZ

WEBER

989-48

ALLEGRO from the OVERTURE IN ITALIAN STYLE

SCHUBERT

ALLEGRO from the OVERTURE to OBERON

WEBER

989-48

FINGAL'S CAVE OVERTURE

ALLEGRO from the CARNIVAL OVERTURE

DVORAK

989-48

ALLEGRO MAESTOSO from the THIRD SYMPHONY

MENDELSSOHN

The Cross-Stick Stroke

In executing rapid passages of symphonic scores it is sometimes convenient to cross one stick over the other in order to maintain a smooth, steady rhythm. However, such style of playing should not be used excessively; neither should it be used as a means of flashy showmanship. A skilled tympanist uses the cross-stick beat sparingly and with discretion.

> Practice Cross-Stick exercises slowly at first, counting four beats to each measure. Then play them faster and faster until you can play them in regular Alla-Breve (cut) time.

x = Cross the next stroke over the last one.